CeLeBRaTe!
in
CeNTRaL AMeRiCa

BY JOE VIESTI AND DIANE HALL
PHOTOGRAPHED BY JOE VIESTI

LOTHROP, LEE & SHEPARD BOOKS • MORROW
NEW YORK

Just as people do in the United States, people in Central America come together to celebrate holidays with song and dance, food and fun, parades and prayer. But the holidays and the ways in which they are celebrated often seem very different from our own. Almost everyone in Central America is Catholic, and most holidays have religious significance, even if they are secular celebrations as well. Almost everyone in Central America is also *mestizo*—a person of mixed Spanish and Indian ancestry. Throughout Central America individual communities have integrated Spanish and Indian traditions in different ways to create their own unique fiestas. But whatever and whenever the celebration, it is always a time to forget about workaday routines and to appreciate the really important things in life: family, beliefs, and traditions. What better way to meet the people of the world than at a celebration!

A shy angel graces a flower-covered float in the Holy Week procession in Nahuizalco, El Salvador.

GUATEMALA

EL DÍA DE LOS MUERTOS

(THE DAY OF THE DEAD)

Many Catholics believe that on November 1, All Saints' Day, the spirits of the dead revisit their earthly homes. Throughout Latin America the holiday is known as *El día de los muertos,* the Day of the Dead. Every year on this day, families gather to tend their relatives' graves and make offerings of food and flowers to welcome them home. Properly honoring the dead is believed to ward off illness, bad luck, and failed crops for the rest of the year.

In Santiago de Sacatepéquez, Guatemala (Santiago for short), people get up at sunrise on November 1 to decorate every door and window of their homes with bright orange marigolds and to prepare offerings of food and drink for their ancestors. Then they head for the hillside cemetery to decorate the graves of their loved ones. Later in the day, as the wind picks up, huge tissue-paper kites fill the skies over the cemetery. Each kite is ten to twenty feet in diameter and requires four or five strong young men to control it. (The young men take the opportunity to impress the young women of the village with their skill and strength.) The kites are flown all afternoon, until the wind dies down at sunset. They will brighten the sky again on November 2, All Souls' Day. Later, they will be burned to honor the spirits of the dead.

A family mausoleum is decorated with a fresh coat of paint and wreaths of flowers and cypress leaves for All Saints' Day (also called All Hallows' Day). In some other cultures, a "day of the dead" is celebrated on October 31, which is All Hallows' Eve—Halloween.

El día de los muertos is celebrated throughout Central America and Mexico. But the huge tissue-paper kites are flown only by the people of Santiago de Sacatepéquez.

GUATEMALA

EL BAILE DE LA CONQUISTA

(THE DANCE OF THE CONQUISTADORS)

At special times during the year the main plaza of the market town of Chichicastenango, in Guatemala's western highlands, is taken over by *El baile de la conquista,* the Dance of the Conquistadors. Elaborately costumed and masked characters perform a choreographed historical pageant commemorating the Spanish conquest of the Maya in the sixteenth century.

Guatemala is the only Central American country with a large Indian population. Forty-four percent of all Guatemalans are Mayan Indians, and they are proud of their heritage. Many Indian women dress as they have for centuries—in colorful handwoven clothing—not just on holidays, but every day. And nowhere is this pride more in evidence than in Chichicastenango, a center of Mayan culture.

El baile de la conquista **is enacted throughout Guatemala to celebrate special occasions.**

(ABOVE) The Moors of North Africa conquered Spain in the eighth century, and their descendants were among the Spanish soldiers who later conquered Guatemala. Some *baile de la conquista* masks are black-faced to represent the Moorish conquistadors. (RIGHT) Some dancers wear plumed and beaded Mayan headdresses that represent conquistador helmets; others wear multicolored sombreros. The wide-brimmed sombrero's name comes from the Spanish word for "shade," *sombra*.

BELIZE

CARNIVAL

Carnival, which occurs every February or March, celebrates the Christian holiday of Shrove Tuesday, better known as Mardi Gras, or Fat Tuesday. This is the last day before Lent, the forty days between Ash Wednesday and Easter Sunday, when Catholics traditionally give up favorite foods and pastimes. In many countries around the world, carnival is a totally uninhibited party before the long Lenten fast begins. Anything goes during carnival!

In San Pedro—a small town on Ambergris Caye, which is the largest of the Belizean barrier islands—carnival lasts for three days. Strolling costumed players fill the dusty, sun-baked streets with music and dancing. Wherever an audience gathers, they stop to perform minimusicals called *comparsas*, especially in front of shops, where the shopkeepers pay them to entertain. Then on Mardi Gras night, prizes are awarded for the best *comparsas*.

In the past, *comparsa* performers would paint their faces and arms as part of their costumes. Then other people started painting themselves, just for fun. Today it's the children who coat one another (and anyone else they can find) with a mixture of paint, flour, and raw egg. During carnival the streets of San Pedro overflow with merry people splashed with color from head to toe.

(ABOVE) **A troupe of young folk dancers step lively for a gathering crowd. Performers of all ages compete for the** *comparsa* **prize. (LEFT) These children have just spotted someone to splatter with their pop bottles full of pastel paints.**

SEMANA SANTA

(HOLY WEEK)

The week before Easter is celebrated with great fervor throughout the tiny country of El Salvador, where it is known as *semana santa*, or Holy Week. This Christian holiday, which occurs every March or April, commemorates the last days in the life of Jesus, his death by crucifixion on Good Friday, and his resurrection on Easter Sunday. Throughout Central America, Good Friday is the holiest day of all.

The town of Sonsonate in western El Salvador was founded in 1552 by conquistadors, who brought with them the Catholic religion, as well as Spanish customs that are still practiced today. One custom is to decorate the streets with *alfombras* for the Good Friday procession. All day Thursday, people of all ages kneel in the streets to create these "carpets," using sawdust, pine needles, flowers, and powdered dyes. The brightly colored *alfombras* depict everything from Mayan Indian symbols to favorite cartoon characters—whatever inspires the artists.

On Good Friday, costumed townspeople reverently re-create the journey of Jesus to his execution. Priests, people in biblical costumes, and teams carrying statues of Jesus and the town's patron saints slowly make their way through streets jammed with spectators. After the procession and crowds have passed, nothing is left of the *alfombras* but trampled petals and swirls of colors in the dust.

(ABOVE) One family has created a cheerful cartoon penguin *alfombra* to brighten the route for the Good Friday procession. (RIGHT) This young artist's *alfombra* urges spectators to let Jesus into their hearts.

EL SALVADOR

EL SALVADOR

Hundreds of townspeople donate their time and talents to present the Good Friday passion play: a reenactment of the events leading up to Jesus' crucifixion. (THIS PAGE) In the village square, costumed "Romans" dramatize Jesus' trial before Pontius Pilate. (FACING PAGE) Teams of strong men (wearing the purple kerchiefs) take turns carrying a heavy statue of Jesus through the streets of Sonsonate.

SAN JOSÉ FAIR

Every year from March 15 to 20, the Honduran village of Copán Ruinas, located near the Guatemalan border, holds a fair in honor of its patron saint, San José (Saint Joseph).

Copán Ruinas is named for the spectacular ruins of the Mayan city of Copán, less than a mile away. The villagers take pride in both their Spanish and Mayan heritages, and the San José fair mixes elements borrowed from both cultures. For five days, food and craft booths pack Copán Ruinas's main plaza. Colorful piñatas, filled with treats, dangle above eager children waiting impatiently for their turn to attack. In the cool of the evening, folk dancers and musicians entertain the crowds.

On the morning of March 19—the Catholic feast day of San José—the entire village gathers to honor its patron saint. Everyone attends a special outdoor mass. Then as a band plays briskly, the statue of San José, dressed in a straw hat and black cape, is carried through mobbed streets. That night, the people of Copán Ruinas wind up the celebration with theatrical performances based on ancient Mayan rituals.

(ABOVE) Copán was a great Mayan city-state that flourished for close to two thousand years. Around 900 A.D. it mysteriously collapsed, leaving massive monuments to be taken over by the jungle. (RIGHT) Whack! A little girl swings with all her might to break the piñata and release its sweet shower of candy.

HONDURAS

HONDURAS

The preservation of both ancient Mayan and Spanish cultures through performance is an important part of the San José fair.

VIRGIN OF MASAYA CELEBRATION

The town of Masaya rests in the shadow of the great double-crested Volcán Masaya. On March 16, 1772, the volcano erupted, threatening to destroy the town. In an act of great courage and faith, the local priest removed a statue of the Virgin Mary from the church and frantically carried her up and down the streets of Masaya. As local people tell the story, the sky suddenly became dark and cloudy and it started to rain, putting an end to the volcanic fires about to engulf the town. It was considered a great miracle, and every year on March 16 the miracle is remembered and celebrated.

First thing in the morning, a group of local women arrives at the church to dress the Virgin and adorn her with flowers. After the statue is robed, the townspeople stream by, touching a hand or foot to receive her blessing. Then the Virgin of Masaya is veiled, placed atop a platform covered by a canopy, and carried up and down the cobbled streets, much as she was in 1772. The whole town joins the parade, marching to the music of a simple brass band.

Despite the natural disasters and bloody warfare that have frequently plagued Nicaragua, the Virgin of Masaya celebration has been held every year since 1772.

(ABOVE) The village of Masaya rests beside a crater lake beneath the great double-crested Volcán Masaya. One of the craters is still active and constantly spews smoke and steam. (LEFT) There is a small burn mark on the delicate hand of the statue, and everyone in Masaya says it was caused by the 1772 volcanic eruption.

COLUMBUS DAY

Columbus Day is celebrated every October 12 throughout the Americas. On this day in 1492, the Italian explorer Christopher Columbus, sailing for Spain's Queen Isabella and King Ferdinand, landed in the Bahamas and "discovered" the Americas for Europe. In many Latin American countries, including Costa Rica, the holiday is also called *El día de la raza,* or "the Day of the Race," for the new race of people, called *mestizo,* created from the intermarriage of arriving Europeans with native peoples.

Thousands of visitors pour into Puerto Limón (also called Limón) for Columbus Day, which often turns into several days of raucous parades and music, singing, and dancing in the streets. The holiday is celebrated with particular enthusiasm in Limón because Columbus landed less than a mile from here on September 18, 1502, during his fourth and final voyage to the Americas. He stayed for seventeen days, noticed that some of the natives wore magnificent gold ornaments, and named the place Costa Rica, meaning "rich coast."

Many people of African ancestry have made their homes along the Caribbean coast of Central America. In Puerto Limón, Costa Ricans of African ancestry celebrate their contribution to the country's rich mix of cultures during the Columbus Day festivities.

COSTA RICA

PANAMA

CARNIVAL

Carnival is a major holiday in many countries in Europe and the Americas, but each nation brings its own special style to the Mardi Gras celebration. In Panama, the old colonial town of Las Tablas was settled by conquistadors in the sixteenth century, and its people preserve many Spanish traditions to this day. Panama's national costume for women, the elegant *pollera,* is of Spanish origin. Most of these intricately embroidered ruffled dresses are made just outside Las Tablas and are to be seen in all their glory there.

Pollera-clad women of all ages are everywhere you look during carnival: in beauty pageants, on parade floats, and dancing in the streets among the throngs who flock to Las Tablas for four days and nights of nonstop partying. Panama is close to the equator, so even though carnival is celebrated in February or March, it's so hot during the day that everyone looks forward to the water fights that break out everywhere.

No matter whether it's satin and sequins or a lacy *pollera*, carnival is a time to dress up in fancy costumes.

(ABOVE) During carnival the party never seems to stop. Night or day, wherever there's a band playing, crowds of people gather. (RIGHT) In the heat of the day, water sprayed from a fire hose offers cooling relief. The crowd screams with glee while being soaked to the bone.

PANAMA

A young dancer works on her moves for a *comparsa* she'll perform for carnival in the town of San Pedro on Ambergris Caye (pronounced *key*), an island off the coast of Belize.

The text type is 14-point Meridien.

Text copyright © 1997 by Joe Viesti and Diane Hall

Illustrations copyright © 1997 by Joe Viesti

Published by Lothrop, Lee & Shepard Books, an imprint of Morrow Junior Books

a division of William Morrow and Company, Inc., 1350 Avenue of the Americas, New York, NY 10019

Printed in Singapore at Tien Wah Press.

1   2   3   4   5   6   7   8   9   10

Library of Congress Cataloging-in-Publication Data

Viesti, Joseph F.

Celebrate! in Central America/by Joe Viesti and Diane Hall; photographed by Joe Viesti.

p. cm.

Summary: Describes the background and customs associated with some of the festivals of Central America.

ISBN 0-688-15161-2 (trade)—ISBN 0-688-15162-0 (library)

1. Festivals—Central America—Juvenile literature.   2. Central America—Social life and customs—Juvenile literature.

[1. Festivals—Central America.   2. Central America—Social life and customs.]

I. Hall, Diane.   II. Title.   GT3933.V54 1997   394.269728—dc21   96-6716   CIP AC